Ashram System

Sampoorna Jeevan, Vadodara

36, Ajitnath Society, Near Water Tank,
Karelibaug, Vadodara- 390018
Ph. No.: 9879293012, 9824351911, 9409306178

E Mail: sampoornajeevanvadodara@gmail.com
Web: www.sjvadodara.co.in
Facebook : https://www.facebook.com/sampoornajeevan.vadodara

Ashram System

Writer, Printer, Publisher

Sampoorna Jeevan, Vadodara
36, Ajitnath Society, Near Water Tank,
Karelibaug, Vadodara- 390018
Ph. No.: 9879293012, 9824351911, 9409306178
E Mail: sampoornajeevanvadodara@gmail.com
Web: www.sjvadodara.co.in
Facebook :
https://www.facebook.com/sampoornajeevan.vadoddara

1st Edition : December, 2022

Ashram System

The word Ashram means to remain blissful while performing our duties at every stage (burdenless life). In this sense, our life is an ashram. The main aim of human life is to reach the highest possible level of fulfilment and development. Ashram system helps one in planning to achieve this aim. Just as one can be successful in every field by proper planning, similarly to succeed in life, one has to plan his lifespan properly. Due to lack of spiritual education, power, prestige and prosperity have become goals for majority of people. This may be considered a success, but it brings anxiety, stress and even depression. Life can be meaningful only when one accomplishes what is required of him (self-realization).

Scriptures proclaim that a human being has to perform four purusharths namely: Dharm, Arth, Kaam and Moksha. Ancient rushis performed extensive penance and lived in peace. They realized importance of Ashrams and gave man the key to live happily for a hundred years by doing karma. They proposed life to be divided into four stages or Ashrams.

The four Ashrams are :

1. From the time of birth to the time one gains capability to earn a living, thereby learning to live a fulfilled life - a period of about one to twenty-five years from birth is **Brahmacharyashram.** During this stage, one gets basic education in both materialistic and spiritual fields, competence in selected skills and necessary physical abilities.
2. After the stage of Brahmacharyashram, one takes responsibility for the spouse, children and other family members, making arrangements for sustenance and providing for future of all family members. This duration, up to a lifespan of about fifty-sixty years is **Gruhasthashram.**
3. To reach the ultimate goal of life, to merge with the manifested form of Paramatma, by performing selfless public service, giving time for its organizational work to run for a lifetime, a duration of life upto age of 75 years is **Vanprasthashram.**
4. Finally to cultivate a state of mind to merge into the formless (unmanifested) Paramatma and easily drift towards end of life by practising sadhana, is **Sannyastashram.** This ashram is to remove all the accumulated desires from one's conscience.

These four phases of lifespan are called **"Ashram system"**

Paramatma's arrangement:

We are fortunate to be born as human beings.

Paramatma has blessed man with developed mind, intellect, chitt and discretion. A person can achieve ascension using them judiciously. The ultimate goal of human life is salvation. Salvation during one's lifetime means eternal bliss. Since Paramatma resides in every human being, a human being has immense potential. He can become Narayan (extraordinary by efforts). As in every field of material life, sound planning is essential to excel in spiritual realm as well.

The rushi-munis meditated and clarified two forms of Paramatma before man. One is a self-fulfilling, invisible, formless Brahmatattva, which is unmanifested and the other is manifested or Saguna-Sakar Swarup, all the Panchmahabhoots and the creatures.

In material field, scientists discovered some basic physical principles and applied them through technology to develop resources so that human labour is reduced and life has become materially rich. Likewise, ancient rushis discovered basic principles in spiritual realm. According to the principle of manifestation, Paramatma manifested Himself as blissful and He created the universe. This means that the whole universe is created from bliss and its purpose is to keep the entire universe in bliss.

According to this principle, Paramatma developed different qualities in human being according to his age for him to live in bliss in all four ashrams.

- The child is innocent, instinctive, simple.
- The youth are hardworking, responsible and diligent.
- Elders become mature & organized and are attracted to spiritual education and understanding of Paramatma.

Basic Truths:

Before we consider how each ashram keeps one in blissful state (duties of human beings in each ashram), let us understand some basic facts:

1. The Principle of Karma clearly establishes that man has to perform karma every moment for a hundred years or as long as he lives, as there is no substitute for karma. The human body is designed in such a way that it can not survive without performing some karma even for a moment. One who leaves karma cannot stay healthy. During every stage of life, human beings must be active, otherwise, their physical and mental health deteriorates and they will suffer from a variety of diseases.
2. Physical and mental changes occur naturally with age. Accordingly, the psyche of man also changes and his work patterns should also change.
3. Blissful Paramatma Himself has manifested as creation. He is omnipresent and spreads joy everywhere. The whole purpose of creation is to spread bliss.
4. There is a clear distinction between humans and other creatures in the ecosystem.

   Only wise and prudent human beings do the right deeds and attain ascension through sadhana. Ultimate goal of a human being is to be happy throughout his entire lifetime, merge into Brahmatattva and attain moksha.
5. Paramatma manages the universe through creatures by an automatic system with complete control over it.
6. The flow of life continues even after the death of the

earthly body of a human being, as the soul is immortal. Jeev gets rebirth either in higher or lower species according to his karma. It carries its experiences, desires, temperaments, habits, beliefs, etc. in its conscience with it, which gives shape to his new birth habits and the journey ahead. In Kath Upanishad, rushi has explained this very beautifully.

Now let us gradually understand the four ashrams according to age groups, keeping in mind the above basic facts.

1. Brahmacharyashram

Jeevatma assumes new birth as a child along with his package of past karma and desires. However, the memories of previous lives are forgotten. What a unique plan of Paramatma ! The receptivity of a human child is vert high. He is innocent and stressless. In those early years, he can be educated properly by his parents, family, teachers and society. The baby is like a new growing plant. He learns from everything around him. It is the responsibility of parents, grandparents and society to nurture him properly.

In Mundak Upanishad Mundak-1, Volume-1, Verse-4, it is clearly explained that human lifespan from five to twenty-five years should be utilized for materialistic and spiritual education to make life meaningful. In ancient times, the child was sent to receive education in gurukul. Today we send him to school. One should acquire thorough knowledge of at least one field to get a job or vocation for sustenance of one's future life. One who expects more, should spend more years in education to become an expert in a subject. It takes about 25 years to gain knowledge for taking responsibilities as a householder to obtain food, clothing and shelter. Then only the phase of Brahmacharyashram is completed.

During Brahmacharyashram, a person depends on parents, family, society and government. This ashram is the foundation of a person's life. Stronger and richer the foundation, better the future life. During these years, along with materialistic education, if one gets spiritual knowledge also, he will become a calm, cultured, tolerant, polite and disciplined citizen.

During Brahmacharyashram, if a person gets knowledge of Jeev, Jagat, Brahm and Atma-Paramatma, then he understands self-realization, self-duty, morality, devotion, religiousness and spirituality. As a result, he becomes more understanding, rational and prepares to be a responsible citizen.

In Brahmacharyashram, one has to solve a question paper of 100 marks, where 50 marks are for materialistic education and 50 marks are for spiritual education and one has to pass in both parts individually. If a balanced knowledge of both spiritual and materialistic fields is provided in Brahmacharyashram, rest of the ashrams become stable, prosperous, successful, dignified and joyful. A wise, calm, thoughtful, productive, compact and conciliatory society is created, which is the necessity in today's world.

Health in Brahmacharyashram :

It is said, "Prevention is better than cure". If it becomes a routine from childhood to have a proper diet, physical exertion, exercise, proper and timely sleep, a person's body remains healthy. If he stays away from addictions, he will have to seek less help from doctors.

2. Gruhasthashram

The first responsibility of a person in Gruhasthashram is to find an appropriate job or vocation to make a living. Only then can he consider getting married. At the same time, he accepts responsibility to serve his parents and elders and maintain his family. He is also expected to procreate to help in nature's plan. Every couple is an important unit of society to become ideal husband-wife, maintaining a variety of relationships as a child and parent and fulfilling their past life's debts.

Gruhasthashram is the nurturer of people living in the other three ashrams.

Gruhasthashram is a test of a young person's intelligence, hard work and discretion. There is no scope for escapism. Gruhasthashram built on a solid foundation of Brahmacharyashram becomes sound and meaningful.

Nature also motivates the body and mind of a twenty-five-year-old youth to move forward as planned by Paramatma. Gruhasthashram is to be utilized for two of the four Purusharths namely Arth and Kaam.

At this stage, every man and woman need to acquire specific knowledge. Proper information and knowledge should be obtained before planning maternity / paternity. It is necessary to understand embryology and the scriptural knowledge of the sixteen sacraments (16 sanskar). Parents' education and training in this subject tune the child's mind. By doing so, the child becomes truthful, non-violent, just, sincere and charismatic. Parents should do intelligent penance for this.

Vocation:

The householder should choose a vocation which suits his nature and where he does not have to carry out any wrong practices, violence or exploitation of others. His livelihood should not depend on others' suffering. If It is so, it is considered Vikam karma, sin and such karma is a binding karma. Moreover, a householder's career should not be contrary to public life, pollute environment or enter into conflict with administration. Thus harmony is maintained and he can live in peace. This is the essence of Agnividya described in Kath Upanishad.

Personality:

Ideal householder is good-natured, self-confident, does not feel hatred, jealousy or revenge against anyone and has a broad vision. He becomes an honourable citizen. He has a love for omnipresent Paramatma.

If a gruhastha keeps on updating his spiritual knowledge received during his Brahmacharyashram, he can easily enter Vanprasthashram.

Financial planning done in Gruhasthashram makes one self-sufficient in later ashrams.

One should not give up income generation activity even if one has good savings in Gruhasthashram.

A misunderstanding:

There is a misconception that when a person earns his livelihood to maintain himself and his family, he is performing sakam karma. So long as one earns his livelihood by working honestly and diligently, without craving to earn beyond his needs and without desire to acquire power, position or prosperity, it is nishkam karma. Rushi gives a clear understanding of this in Chapter-1, Valli-1, Verse-18 of Kath Upnishad. Human beings get closer to Paramatma by being moral, religious and spiritual while earning a livelihood. Conscience becomes pure through this kind of work. Thus, if every action is performed as a worship, it becomes Nishkam karma and builds character. Such a person can be consistently happy while handling worldly responsibilities of a householder.

Requirement:

We feel sorry learning about dishonesty and corrupt behaviour of majority of people in society. The reason is absence of spiritual education. Though being clever and intelligent, even capable human beings slip into love for power, prestige and prosperity on account of lack of spiritual education (Paravidya). So their chariot of life does not climb to the path of Devayan. They do not remain in a blissful state themselves and they cannot make others happy.

Paramatma has given man a life longer than most of the creatures in the ecosystem. Yet most people in society live animalistic lives because of lack of spiritual education. So, a few wise great men have to work harder. Due to prevalence of materialistic education, most people work only to earn a living to have material prosperity in the world. Similarly, if each citizen performs proper deeds as per his ashram, world peace will prevail expanding the realm of joy everywhere.

3. Intermission

Till now, we discussed Brahmacharyashram and Gruhasthashram. Most people have understanding of these two ashrams. Many people are living successfully in both these ashrams. Rushi adds two more aspects, acquring spiritual education along with materialistic education in Brahmacharyashram and practising Agnividya in Gruhasthashram. This means performing one's karma as worship. In it, rushi says that purity of environment should be maintained and every creature should remain happy, while any professional activity is done.

The two ashrams of the second part of life - Vanaprastha and Sannyast Ashram are not understood fully even by people in higher economic, professional, political and social positions. . As a result, both senior citizens and society are losers. Most people seek rest and pleasure in remaining life,

There is a big misunderstanding in society about two subjects. The first is that all arrangements of public life should be handled only by government. The government can collect more taxes, but it is its responsibility to ensure a comfortable life for all citizens. Such a belief is harmful to society as a whole.

Another popular belief is that as senior citizens have exhausted themselves in Gruhasthashram, they should rest now as they are not physically fit. They should enjoy what they have not been able to do in their working life. They should perform Bhajan-Kirtan, Satsang, Yatras, travels, look after their grand-children etc... Organizations for senior citizens also carry out such activities and believe that this will bring happiness to their members. This is contrary to the principle of karma.

Both the above beliefs are contrary to the ideologies of our rushis. A comparative study of various ideologies reveals that the system propagated by rushis is still rational and relevant today.

Due to current democratic governance systems, corruption in government and public sector is so widespread that, from one hundred rupees of the budgets of government schemes, the real benefit to citizens is only fifteen rupees. Rest of the amount is shared between officials and political leaders. If sincere senior citizens/vanprasths are involved in certain areas and they shoulder responsibility selflessly, government can be replaced in this kind of work, corruption can be largely eradicated. Burden on tax-payers can also be reduced.

Most senior citizens stop working after retirement. As a result, seniors have a higher incidence of physical and mental diseases. Insurance companies are not ready to undertake insurance of elders because of such half-truths. Nowhere In Ayurveda, it is mentioned that people get sick due to old age. Ayurveda states that active life is essential to remain healthy till the last breath of life.

A senior citizen who remains absorbed in selfless public life, his physical and mental health definitely improve. Moreover, his conscience gets purified because of his selfless activities and his happiness increases progressively.

Rushi clarifies two forms of Paramatma before us. One is Parabrahma Paramatma, which is formless and unmanifested. His second form is manifestation in the form of gross creation.

All species except humans do not have a developed mind. So they behave as per their instincts. They play the role as decided for them by Paramatma. They travel through various species (yoni) one by one and eventually are born as human beings. They are not bound by their Karma. However, man is free to do any karma as per his wishes, but he is bound by the principle of Karma.

By creating sound systems of public life, senior citizens can help to create a beautiful world. Tireless work of many great men has resulted in a world physically fit to live happily.

Worship of the manifested form of Paramatma means helping Him to maintain world order by determining our role to sustain it properly. It is the responsibility of a Gruhasth to provide all the required essentials to everyone in the society to lead a happy personal life. He is supposed to manufacture or produce, sell, distribute and provide services accordingly. A well-established economic structure already exists for this. On the other hand, for vanprasthas to do their job properly, they need a public infrastructure as a base, which can be developed and maintained by

Vanprasthas (Elders/ Senior citizens). Elders have experience, they can build an organization very easily by working hard and honestly. The government can become less burdened if responsibility is shared by elders. Elders can serve in many fields like Hygiene, Education, Rural Development, Research etc.

Let us understand these two Ashrams of second innings in life in detail; The word "Vanaprastha Ashram" is derived from beautiful arrangements from the time of rushis. The forests were uninhabited at that time. Small states were having limited boundaries. Seniors migrated to nearby forests in small groups when their children became self-reliant. They acquired land from forest and built ashram on it. This was known as Vanprasthashram (Van +prasthan). They mainly engaged in educational activity. They were self-sufficient. They did farming, manufactured clothes, constructed houses and disciples helped in it. They taught the disciples all essential sciences, arts and skills of life as well as imparted spiritual knowledge. They did this without burdening the Gruhasthas. In short, they helped in social activities which were useful to family and professional life as well as society.

In the spiritual realm, it is the essence which matters. Let us therefore determine the role of vanprastha in today's world.

4. Vanprasthashram

A person in Brahmacharyashram lives on support from his parents, teachers and society. He is bound by family and vocation in Gruhasthashram. But in Vanprasthashram, he gets the opportunity to get beyond the family life and be helpful in social work. He needs funds and accummulation of resources (Parigraha) for material success in Gruhasthashram. However, in Vanprasthashram to be spiritual, he has to practise non-accumulation (aparigraha).

Gruhastha gradually hands over responsibilities for his family and business to his children or heirs and shifts towards duty to society. He joins suitable organization and engages himself in public welfare tasks. At this stage, Paravidya's knowledge gives him the strength to serve others. He begins to live spiritual life. The Vanaprastha sees Paramatma in every Jeeva, so it is a pleasure to do social work without any hesitation. His thoughts and personality change. He no longer insists on his own notions. He accepts everyone, so he is also accepted by all. He shares his skills, knowledge and experience unhesitatingly with others in society. He enjoys this endlessly from his heart.

Children of a senior person become Gruhasthas and take over responsibilities of business and family and he can become a Vanaprastha. However, he need not leave his home and family when it comes to serving the wider world. He continues to serve elderly parents and guide children and gives emotional support to his spouse so their bond becomes stronger. He becomes dearer to everyone including Paramatma.

Vanaprastha has an unwavering determination to live a satisfied and contented life for a hundred years by utilizing the knowledge of Paravidya and doing selfless service. Nature will also support his decision and his routine, diet, exercise, rest and sleep patterns will also change. His financial conditions may vary, but his self-confidence and decision-making will not be affected by them. He will be able to spare 3-4 hours daily for activities for public welfare. As he remains active, he ages slowly. He will be young at heart and will not be dependent on anyone for his daily needs.

Organization for senior citizens:

On graduation from college, a deserving young person gets a job directly from the college campus. The company trains him as per its needs and the person utilizes his knowledge and skills to earn his livelihood. Everyone may not be capable of developing his own business. If industrial infrastructure is not developed, jobs will be scarce and they will not be able to earn their livelihood. Similarly, there must be an organization for senior citizens who have experience of nearly five decades and want to serve society selflessly. There is no dearth of work for an experienced and knowledgeable person. This kind of organization can keep track of public services required by social service organizations, industries, government departments and institutions and inform the registered Vanprastha members. This organization should also take care that the Vanprasthas get work of their choice, close to their residence for a convenient period. Such an organization can be an employment exchange for Vanprasthas. It will also technically upgrade skills of Vanaprasthas where necessary. Such a structure is not available today for Vanprasthas. It needs to be developed.

Sadly, long years of slavery and blind imitation of the West have developed a system where just when an adult gets a real grip on work and thorough knowledge of his job, it is time for him to retire, sit idle and depend on pension. This culture has affected adversely both society as well as the elderly citizens. Physical and mental exercise is a must for a person to live a healthy and joyful life. A person loses both health and confidence if he does not find his life to be useful and meaningful. Mental illnesses such as dementia, Parkinson's and Alzheimer's diseases can also occur. He can also lose respect from his family and society in general. What to do after sixty years of life is a question every senior citizen strives to get an answer. Such organizations should be created at city, district and state level as required.

A man does not have an impact on society so long as he does not live the life of a Vanprashtha. Karma is the best means of attaining bliss. To understand this, one has to continuously update one's spiritual knowledge.

The elders need activities similar to what they did in Gruhasthashram but they need to perform them selflessly for betterment of society as a whole. This way they can get respect in society and internal happiness . Jeev is a part of Anandghan Paramatma, so he wants bliss on a continuous basis. He will fail if he tries to find happiness in wrong places and this may lead to depression. Those who are not trained spiritually in first two Ashrams in early life, go through this kind of situation later in life. This condition is visible in any senior citizen group.

Nishkam karma can be performed in commercial and industrial establishments, but it is a little difficult. Charitable and service-minded organizations can do these types of work easily. The new structure would create a bridge between Vanprasthas and Charitable organizations.

Opportunity to absolve past debts:

Human life and all relationships are founded on the basis of debts of many entities. The first is that of Paramatma, who gave one birth as a human being. So love the Lord, worship Him, sing His praise, trust Him fully, have full faith and do work which He will like.

The second debt is towards parents, who brought us into this world, gave us the sacraments (sanskar), education and raised us. Give them time, serve them, respect them and help them in every way. Similarly, love your spouse and your children. Support them in their joys and sorrows. Be friendly with them and give them due respect.

The third is the debt towards the Rushi-munis. The knowledge that was penned for us through penance is saved in the Satshastras. We should faithfully follow the scriptures to pay tribute to them. We need to read, understand, meditate, put that knowledge into practice and share it with others.

The fourth debt is of the society. How many peoples' services we all have availed of in our lifetime ? We cannot live happily without them. We can do social work and by joining the right organization, we can do it more systematically.

Finally comes Mother Earth's debt, which nourishes our body through grain, air, water etc. We need to take care that Mother Earth can be healthy for years to come by reducing pollution and conserving the environment.

In the first Mundak of Mundak Upanishad, Volume-2, Verse-11, Rushi specifically says that the person who does not clear these debts in his Vanprasthashram is not eligible to enter Brahmalok.

Training senior citizens:

Most social organizations in society have dual standards. This is because of the very low rate of spiritual education. As a result, even the senior persons in their current management, use the same materialistic methods. If we want our senior citizens to be trained to become Vanprashtha in true sense, we have to provide them proper and systematic training.

1. According to the existing system, most citizens work for power, prestige and prosperity. Vanaprastha Ashram is the stage for approaching Paramatma where power, prestige and prosperity do not affect them. Senior citizens who have achieved a level of contentment are the ones, who are ready to become Vanaprastha. They receive energy from the soul and perform activities for their personal bliss. They feel that they have gathered a lot and now it is time to renounce as much as possible and reduce consumption.
2. Material organizations have different levels, such as Supervisor, Manager, Director, Chairman etc. Vanprashtha organizations do not have such levels.

   In the materialistic realm, one earns money which comes from external sources. In Vanaprasthashram,by performing selfless service, one earns bliss which comes from within and is eternal. True Vanprastha can show the path to others for getting into that state. Bliss exists within everyone. Vanaprastha person will help everyone to eliminate hurdles and reach bliss.
3. Area of influence: Householders and senior citizens get impressed by dignitaries in their respective fields. They rearrange systems according to their likes and dislikes. However, a Vanprastha person is neither trying to impress others, nor does he get impressed by anyone, as he has reached a higher level of spirituality. Hence, the systems are developed according to requirements of the job and not individuals.

4. Vanprasth also has to work like a Gruhastha. The difference is that instead of self,family or professional arrangements, he is now involved in social activities for others' benefit. For this, he needs a special type of training. He needs to keep pace with new technologies such as computers, digitization etc.
5. Since a Gruhastha is engaged in a limited field of vocational activity, he only knows his own subject. A Vanprastha needs to learn many disciplines of work, as he will be working in several areas of an organization. Moreover, he has to develop a habit of consulting his colleagues to take decisions jointly. He needs to delegate work to others and control at the level of soul. Every Vanprastha needs a special type of training to inculcate these habits.

Surprising Fact:

Today, there are an estimated 200 million senior citizens in India. Against this, there are only 50 million employees in government and public service. If retired senior citizens provide service in the fields of their skills just for two hours a day, several government activities can be taken over by Vanprasthas. This can lighten the burden on the youth and the government. This will make work of charitable organizations easier, reduce corruption and bring about a higher level of efficiency. Society benefits from loving and emotional public order. This is the influence of spiritual knowledge.

There are so many doctors, engineers, lawyers, officers and businessmen who have retired and are physically fit to work. If they are engaged in selfless service to society according to their knowledge and skills, they can help the country and humanity in a big way. If seniors get active in social work, prevailing economic inequality can be kept within limits. This can be done in all fields.

Seniors who do not leave their business due to mistrust of younger generation's abilities or attachment to business, are ruining their own and others' lives. They have not understood spirituality. This is the most important phase of life which can be the most enjoyable too. This phase is to prepare oneself for sannyatashram. In both Vanprasthashram and Sanyastashram one has to be active. Only the way it is done, changes. In this phase, one is active to serve others and not for monetary benefits.

Three careers of a person:

Understanding knowledge, duty and swadharma in Brahmacharyashram is preparation for a man's first career. Aitareya Upanishad calls it the first birth of a man. Taking responsibility for family in Gruhasthashram, giving proper education and sacraments to children by making them honest and responsible citizens is fulfilment of a man's second career, his second birth. Gradually handing over family and business responsibilities to successors and entering Vanprasthashram, engaging in service of Paramatma by getting involved in public life in a selfless manner, is the third career, i.e. the third birth of a man. In this way, Spiritual education helps a person to take responsibility for family and society willingly with a happy frame of mind.

Caution:

It is necessary to take care not to sacrifice family life for social work during Vanaprasthashram. One's family is also part of society. Sometimes his services may be needed in business.

In times of recession, legal entanglement or sickness, he must guide the new generation in times of crisis. Responsibilities renounced earlier may also have to be re-assumed until the crisis gets over.

Doing light chores at home, helps keep one healthy and happy.

Many saints, mahatmas and devotees have fulfilled their family and business liabilities while serving Paramatma. Same is true for Vanprastha person. How can one become detached from one's family?

Inheritance of property is to be given to his children to the extent that they deserve. He can make trusts, sponsor research etc. and can create a perpetual system so that his savings are spent in public interest.

Transformation:

A person in Brahmacharyashram lives on support of his parents, teachers and society. In Gruhasthahram, he has to earn his livelihood to support not only himself and his family, but also those in the other three ashrams i.e. society at large. In this ashram, he is bound by his family and profession.

Towards the end of Gruhasthashram, a person retires from active life willingly or unwillingly. If he is in service, he has to compulsorily retire on attaining age of 58 or 60 years, even though he may be physically and mentally fit. If he is self-employed, he hesitates to hand over reins of his business or profession to his grown-up children or heirs either due to strong attachment or lack of trust in their abilities to shoulder responsibilities and ends up deeply involved in material world for the rest of his life. If decides to retire from active life, he has two choices; 1) To remain active, using his knowledge and experience of material education, to add to his material prosperity or 2) To remain idle and pass time in travelling or spending time with his grandchildren, bidding time for his death.

If he accepts the first choice, he may remain physically and mentally fit, but he may not have inner happiness. In the second case, as his body and mind do not get required exercise, he is soon likely to become infirm and may develop psycho-somatic diseases like Alzeimer's or Parkinson's. He is likely to get frustrated and go into depression. He becomes a burden to ho his family and society and loses their respect.

Today, because of better medical facilities, average life expectancy has increased. Every year more and more senior citizens are added. If an effective system for channelizing their wide knowledge and experience in a selfless manner for benefit of the society at large is not created, burden on the youth in Gruhasthashram and the government increases.

However, if the person has acquired spiritual knowledge right from the beginning of his life, he ensures that during

Gruhasthashram, he acquires sufficient wealth so that he can live independently for the rest of his life. He now gradually hands over his family and professional responsibilities to his grown-up children or heirs.

Through spiritual knowledge, he realizes that Paramatma is present in every particle of universe. His vision is broadened and he understands the principle of Karma. He takes life's events in his stride with equanimity. He now works only for public welfare instead of himself and his family. This helps him to prepare to move easily to Sannyastashram towards the end of his Vanprathashram.

Paramatma himself is Nirgun-Nirakar, but he has manifested Himself as Sagun-sakar in this Universe. Similarly, Atma is Nirgun-Nirakar, but resides in the physical body. If one wants to ultimately attain Moksha or Brahm, it can only be done by utilizing his physical body in a selfless manner for betterment of the material world, which is created by Paramatma Himself. For this, one has to purify one's mind and intellect through Sadhana and Upasana.

Spiritual education guides one towards selfless service at every stage of life to remove the existing impurities of mind and intellect. It also offers age-appropriate convenience like knowledge, karma, yoga and devotion.

Essential:

The person who has learnt Paravidya in Brahmacharyashram, and utilized it in Gruhasthashram, should have clear knowledge and understanding of the following facts while entering Vanprasthashram. If not, he should strive to gain this knowledge in Vanaprasthashram.

1. Philosophical distinction between sect, religion and spirituality.
2. Clear meaning of the words Jeevatma, Atma and Paramatma.
3. Manifested and unmanifested forms of Paramatma.
4. Difference between happiness and bliss.
5. Difference between what he likes and what is good for him (Shreya and Preya).

Senior Citizen	***Vanprasth***
Both are mature and experienced	
Lack of spiritual knowledge	*Educated in spiritual knowledge*
Narrow minded, self-centered	*Broad minded, philanthropic*
Busy in family life	*Engaged in social services*
Longing for happiness in entertainment	*Strives for happiness in selfless service.*
Lazy.	*Active.*
Lack of clear vision.	*Has clear vision*
Has limited goals.	*Higher goals*
Neglected by family and	*Accepted everywhere*
society.	
Smartness.	*Wisdom*
Influenced by Tamas and Rajas gunas	*Predominance of sattvaguna*

5. Sannyastashram

This is the last stage of human life. At this stage too, activity is not to be given up, only the approach changes. Just as the person, who created and nurtured his family and professional organization in Gruhasthashram and handed over responsibilities to heirs and applied his knowledge and abilities to help in social welfare in Vanprasthashram; similarly while moving towards Sannyastashram, he hands over the social activities he was performing, to other vanaprasthas and becomes free of all the materialistic attachments. Any position in the organization is also to be vacated. Then, he has to be ready to only provide guidance when sought, without being active in their daily administration.

For a good social system, all types of institutions are required like family, professional, political, and social organizations. These organizations take years to stabilize. If due to some reason, the organization collapses, then the new generation has to again start the activity from a scratch. This will really be a huge loss. For organizations to be functioning flawlessly and continuously, it is necessary that vanprasths hand over responsibilities in the organization in good time and work indirectly. The person who remains in a position for his own selfish motives, loses respect of his colleagues and at the same time harms the organization.

There are many misconceptions in society about Sannyastashram. In the fifth chapter of the Bhagavad Gita, in verse 6, it is stated that it is easier for a person to follow karmayoga than Sannyas. Yet the second verse of the seighteenth chapter advises to renounce karm for desires, not karma itself. In the fifth verse, it is stated that Yagna, Daan and Tapa karm are not to be renounced. They help to purify oneself.

Sannyastashram is an ashram to prepare for next birth. For a better reincarnation, special efforts have to be put in this final stage. It is also promised that, even if the seeker who strives for Moksha with complete devotion, does not attain Moksha in this birth, he is born into a family with conducive environment, so that he can continue his spiritual journey. When it is completed, he attains Moksha.

The way he devoted time for serving the material form of Brahm in Vanaprashthashram,now the person has to strive to merge in formless Brahm. He has to cultivate his mental attitude accordingly, so that he can die with a smile without any fear. It is time to eradicate desires that are left over from

www.ingramcontent.com/pod-product-compliance
Lightning Source LLC
Chambersburg PA
CBHW022205160726
48282CB00024B/325

* 9 7 8 8 1 9 6 2 7 8 2 5 0 *